YOU

CAN SAVE THE EARTH

YOU

CAN SAVE THE EARTH

7 REASONS WHY &
7 SIMPLE WAYS

A PHILOSOPHY FOR THE FUTURE

hatherleigh

Hatherleigh Press is committed to preserving and protecting the natural
resources of the Earth. Environmentally responsible and sustainable practices are embraced within the company's mission statement.

Hatherleigh Press is a member of the Publishers Earth Alliance, committed to preserving and protecting the natural resources of the planet while
developing a sustainable business model for the book publishing industry.

PEA Member   Recycled Content   Earth-Friendly Printing   Cause Supporting

Recycled Content: The interior of this
book is printed on 100% recycled paper.

Earth-Friendly Printing: The interior
of this book was printed with soy ink.

Cause Supporting

hatherleigh

5-22 46th Avenue, Suite 200
Long Island City, NY 11101
www.hatherleighpress.com

Library of Congress Cataloging-in-Publication Data
You can save the Earth : 7 reasons why & 7 simple ways :
a philosophy for the future.
    p. cm.
    Includes bibliographical references.
    ISBN 978-1-57826-280-9 (pbk.)
    1. Environmental education. 2. Environmental protection—Citizen
participation. I. Hatherleigh Press.
    GE70.Y685 2008
    333.72—dc22

            2008035417ISBN 978-1-57826-280-9

You Can Save the Earth is available for bulk purchase, special promotions,
and premiums. For information on reselling and special purchase opportunities, call 1-800-528-2550 and ask for the Special Sales Manager.

Cover design by Michael Fusco, michaelfuscodesign.com

10 9 8 7 6 5 4 3 2
Printed in the United States

Mankind has long endeavored to reach out to the heavens. We have set foot on the moon, launched probes into the vast depths of space, pondered dwellings in zero gravity. Yet, perhaps all this effort and investment was spent not to find a new home, but rather to turn the cameras around and capture a photo of our Earth. Beautiful, fragile, alive. A solitary Ark carrying us forward through time.

We are at a watershed moment in the history of our world, when we must make the changes required to embrace a sustainable future. The good news is that it's a choice we are free to make, and we should do so with a spirit of optimism.

Consider *You Can Save the Earth* a gift of hope and an enduring message to help safeguard the Earth, its environments, and each other.

—Andrew Flach, Publisher

CONTENTS

"The divine is not something high above us. It is in heaven, it is in earth, it is inside us."

—Morihei Ueshiba

YOU

CAN SAVE THE EARTH

This book is about how you can save the Earth.

The threat to Earth's environment isn't new. But it is more pressing than it has ever been. There is no doubt that our way of living is causing the Earth tremendous damage. This is damage we must stop—for ourselves, and for the generations that will come after us.

However, this book does not contain photographs of polluted skies or trees stripped bare by acid rain or of overflowing landfills. Certainly, you have seen enough of those images.

"Conservation is a state of harmony between men and land . . . harmony with land is like harmony with a friend; you cannot cherish his right hand and chop off his left."

—ALDO LEOPOLD

And if those photos haven't already motivated you, then they never will.

Instead of terrifying you, this book is going to empower you.

Begin by understanding how our lifestyle is affecting the Earth we inhabit. Then, think about why *you* value clear skies, safe water, and a bountiful natural landscape. Suddenly, your own motivation will become clear to you. Once you are ready to act, learn about steps you can take that will truly make a difference for the Earth, and for all of us.

You can save the Earth.

"We, the people, are going to have to put our thoughts together, our power together, to save our planet here. We've only got one water, one air, one Mother Earth."

—CORBIN HARNEY

7 REASONS
WHY

"The love of wilderness is more than a hunger for what is always beyond reach; it is also an expression of loyalty to the earth, the earth which bore us and sustains us, the only paradise we shall ever know, the only paradise we ever need . . . wilderness is not a luxury but a necessity of the human spirit, as vital to our lives as water and good bread."

—EDWARD ABBEY

YOU

CAN SAVE THE EARTH

How is the way we live now affecting the Earth? It's important to understand why our means of transportation, the way we eat, and the energy we consume are changing our environment, so we can protect our planet—our one and only home.

As you learn more about the effect of our habits on the Earth, think about why a healthy environment is important to you. Remind yourself how much you value clean air, clear water, litter-free beaches, fresh food and unspoiled open spaces. Aren't these part of what makes life worth living?

"All that we did, all that we said or sang must come from contact with the soil."

—WILLIAM BUTLER YEATS

Find your own motivation to guard a healthy Earth. Maybe it's because you love to fly fish in sparkling streams. Maybe you're fond of morning bike rides or walking your dog through the woods. Let your own personal experiences guide you.

Listen to your own voice—your own conscience—when you hear more about the state of the environment around the globe.

"If, as the elders have told us, we are our grandparents' dream, then we must today begin dreaming of our grandchildren."

—WALTER BRESETTE

1

ALL OF LIFE IS INTERCONNECTED

"Climate change can affect human health directly (e.g., impacts of thermal stress, death/injury in floods and storms) and indirectly through changes in the ranges of disease vectors (e.g., mosquitoes), water-borne pathogens, water quality, air quality, and food availability and quality."

—WORLD HEALTH ORGANIZATION

ALL OF LIFE on Earth is connected.

A seed needs soil, sun, and water to grow into a vegetable. The vegetable provides our bodies with the energy needed to function and thrive.

We must guard this precious cycle of life by protecting every element at each stage of growth. For, if one step is compromised, we are all at risk.

Here is an example: in April 2006, a toxic cloud of pollution wafted from Northern China, across the Pacific Ocean, to the West Coast of the United States. Meteorologists reported finding residue from this toxic "cloud" atop mountains in California, Oregon, and Washington. When the quality of the air is compromised somewhere in the world, we all pay the price. The Earth does not pay attention to borders or nationalities. This means our neighbor's environmental disasters are also ours.

"There are two principles inherent in the very nature of things, recurring in some particular embodiments whatever field we explore— the spirit of change, and the spirit of conservation. There can be nothing real without both. Mere change without conservation is a passage from nothing to nothing."

—ALFRED NORTH WHITEHEAD

In the United States, 6 billion pounds of phosphorus and nitrogen fertilizers from Midwestern farms leach into the Mississippi and its tributaries every year, causing massive algae blooms. Bacteria consume the algae, depleting the oxygen in the water and literally suffocating all marine life. Then, this toxic soup flows down to the mouth of the Mississippi and into the Gulf of Mexico, where it has created a "dead zone" that now measures almost 7,500 square miles, an area nearly the size of New Jersey. American farm run-off has become an international environmental hazard.

All of life on Earth is connected by actions across time. Our choices today shape the world that our children and grandchildren will inherit. Our descendants rely on us all to preserve our only home and leave it for them in better shape than we found it.

All of us must work to preserve life on Earth. Saving the Earth depends on the cooperation of communities, both locally and

"Soil is a resource, a living, breathing entity that, if treated properly, will maintain itself. It's our lifeline for survival. When it has finally been depleted, the human population will disappear."

—MARJORIE HARRIS

globally. We are all responsible for protecting our air, water, and soil.

Recognizing our interdependence is the first step to saving our planet. We humans have only one home, and we must care for it—together.

EXERCISE:
>   Find a quiet place. Close your eyes for a moment and feel yourself connected to all living things.

AFFIRMATION:
>   *I am connected to life and to our Earth.*

"The first wealth is health."

—Ralph Waldo Emerson

2

THE HEALTH OF
THE EARTH
DEFINES OUR
WELL-BEING

"Today, the world population is encounting unfamiliar human-induced changes in the lower and middle atmospheres and world-wide depletion of various other natural systems. Beyond the early recognition that such changes would affect economic activities, infrastructure and managed ecosystems, there is now recognition that global climate change poses risks to human population health."

—WHO ON CLIMATE CHANGE
AND HUMAN HEALTH

THE HEALTH OF the Earth is vital to our health. If the soil is poisoned, a plant will not grow. If our air is polluted, our health is at risk.

The consequences for our health from global warming and climate change are numerous. The World Health Organization reports, "Climate change can affect human health directly (e.g., impacts of thermal stress, death/injury in floods and storms) and indirectly through changes in the ranges of disease vectors (e.g., mosquitoes), water-borne pathogens, water quality, air quality, and food availability and quality."

Freezes and flooding, and droughts and heat waves, result in multiple deaths and outbreaks of disease. Physical displacement due to cataclysmic weather events (hurricanes, tsunamis) often results in contaminated drinking water supplies which can lead to massive outbreaks of cholera and other waterborne diseases.

As the Earth's temperatures rise, there has

"I would feel more optimistic about a bright future for man if he spent less time proving that he can outwit Nature and more time tasting her sweetness and respecting her seniority."

—ELWYN BROOKS WHITE

been a simultaneous increase in outbreaks of certain heat-related infectious diseases, including malaria, dengue fever, and yellow fever. This occurs often in regions that had not previously seen the diseases—including the United States, where cases of the West Nile virus and Lyme disease have appeared. Air pollution and declining air quality have resulted in a doubling if not a tripling of asthma cases over the past 20 years. Changing weather patterns affect agriculture; threatened crops and livestock can result in widespread undernourishment. Climate and land-use changes, according to the WHO, "are responsible for putting an estimated 40 percent of the world population at risk of contracting malaria, as well as placing 840 million people at risk of malnutrition. A further 1 to 2 billion people living in mid to high latitudes face a higher risk of skin cancer and immune system depression."

Climate change and unstable environment are creating the conditions for a health crisis, one with both long- and short-term consequences.

"The future is knocking at our door right now. Make no mistake, the next generation will ask us one of two questions. Either they will ask, 'What were you thinking; why didn't you act?' or they will ask instead, 'How did you find the moral courage to rise and successfully resolve a crisis that so many said was impossible to solve?'"

—AL GORE

Once, miners used caged canaries to monitor the levels of odorless poisonous gases in mine shafts. If the caged canary was singing and strong, the shaft's air was safe to breathe. But if the canary's song stopped, the miners knew the air was deadly and that they were in grave danger.

Those who are ill because of air pollution and declining air quality are showing us that our health is threatened. This is a warning to us that we must reverse course—that we must reconsider our actions to protect the health of the Earth.

For us to be healthy, our Earth must be healthy. The time has come to protect our health.

EXERCISE:
Gently place your fingers on your pulse and acknowledge the extraordinary miracle of your beating heart.

AFFIRMATION:
I value my health. I value my family's health. I value the Earth's health.

"We forget that the water cycle and the life cycle are one."

—Jacques Cousteau

3

WATER IS
THE ESSENCE OF
ALL LIFE

"Rivers are roads which move,
and which carry us whither
we desire to go."

—Blaise Pascal

WE OFTEN FORGET that our first stages of life unfold "underwater," in the womb.

After we enter the world, water continues to enable our growth. We need water in order to live.

Yet, the *way* we live is threatening this vital resource. Here is an example: bottled water. In 2006, Americans consumed over 31 billion liters of bottled water. Although we are doing our body good by consuming our daily intake of H_2O, purchasing water in plastic bottles is a big mistake for our Earth. For one thing, all those empty bottles end up in already overcrowded landfills. Second, manufacturing those plastic bottles requires the use of an expensive, nonrenewable, and polluting resource: oil. The oil necessary for the production of plastic water bottles topped 17 million barrels in 2006. That's enough oil to fuel more than 1 million cars and trucks *for a whole year*. And all that oil is just

"A river seems a magic thing.
A magic, moving, living part
of the very earth itself."

—LAURA GILPIN

for manufacturing the bottles; even more is required for shipment, delivery, and removal. One estimate holds that it takes a quarter bottle of oil to produce and deliver every bottle of water.

Oil leads to pollution, and the effects of pollution *aren't* just limited to some faraway shore. Pollution has come home, right into the water and onto the shorelines we love to enjoy. Nearly *half* of America's rivers and lakes are too polluted for fishing or swimming. That's because our recreational waters are polluted by over a trillion gallons of untreated sewage, storm water, and industrial waste every year. This also threatens our drinking water supplies, since sewage and industrial waste can leach into our groundwater and wells.

If you take a moment to think about some of the most popular vacation spots around the world, you will probably think of several getaways near a body of water. Oceans, lakes, streams, and waterfalls relax our bodies and cleanse our minds. Whether we seek water to swim, gaze at the waves, or listen to the

"Man is not an aquatic animal, but from the time we stand in youthful wonder beside a spring brook till we sit in old age and watch the endless roll of the sea, we feel a strong kinship with the waters of this world."

—HAL BORLAND

rhythm of the surf, water relieves stress and elevates our state of mind.

Water is a source of healing. We must use this precious element responsibly and guard its cleanliness for our future. It is important not only for the health of our bodies, but for the health of our sprits as well.

We must ensure the future of our clean drinking water, and we must preserve the bodies of water that we so love to admire.

EXERCISE:

Pour yourself a glass of water in a clear container. For a moment, reflect on how your own body is made up of over 50% percent water.

AFFIRMATION:

Water flows within me. I cherish pure water.

"I only went out for a walk
and finally concluded to stay
out till sundown, for going out,
I found, was really going in."

—JOHN MUIR

4

THE AIR WE
BREATHE

"The time has come to lower our voices, to cease imposing our mechanistic patterns on the biological processes of the earth, to resist the impulse to control, to command, to force, to oppress, and to begin quite humbly to follow the guidance of the larger community on which all life depends."

—Thomas Berry

How MANY BREATHS do we take in a day? It would be impossible to count. We cannot live without breathing. Air is our lifeline.

For this reason, we must stop polluting our skies. You know air pollution if you have been on a street crowded with cars, buses, and trucks. Air pollution harms the life around us. But do you know the long-term consequences of this pollution?

Statistics suggest that the United States is responsible for one-fourth of global greenhouse gas emissions, a result of the burning of fossil fuels.

We burn fossil fuels to run our cars and planes (gasoline and oil) and light our homes (electricity). In the United States, fossil fuels provide more than 85 percent of energy. When we burn fossil fuels to produce energy, we generate massive quantities of carbon dioxide and other gases like nitrous oxide, ozone, and methane. Automobile exhaust is

"This most excellent canopy, the air . . . this brave o'erhanging firmament, this majestical roof . . ."

—WILLIAM SHAKESPEARE

95 percent carbon dioxide. This means that the typical passenger vehicle produces over 5 metric tons of carbon dioxide per year. These numbers add up even faster when you look at the energy we burn for planes, trains, and trucks: almost 6 billion metric tons of carbon dioxide annually.

Among other things, heavy pollution in the air causes: human heart and lung disease, including asthma and emphysema, damage to crop plants and trees, sometimes in the form of acid rain, structural damage to some of our national monuments are decaying at rapid rates because of smog from cities and water pollution, when mercury and other heavy metals are absorbed by rivers and ponds. Research indicates that half of all Americans live in areas with unsafe levels of air pollution.

Every one of us needs to be more aware of how much pollution we add to the air. Think about it: when we can no longer see the "purple mountain majesties" of our national anthem, then it's time for a change.

"The Earth is what we all have in common. It is what we are made of and what we live from, and we cannot damage it without damaging those with whom we share it."

—WENDELL BERRY

EXERCISE:

Wherever you are right now, breathe deeply and fully, filling you lungs with air. Exhale slowly. Be conscious of each breath.

AFFIRMATION:

Though invisible, the air I breathe sustains my life. I value fresh, clean air.

"The United States has the world's mightiest economy and most mobile society. Yet the oil that fueled its strength has become its greatest weakness."

—AMORY LOVINS

5

THE LIMITS OF
FOSSIL FUELS

"Oil is seldom found where it is most needed, and seldom most needed where it is found."

—L.E.J. Brouwer

OIL HAS BEEN an essential tool for nearly everything our society has accomplished. Our country's history and that of much of the world, has been shaped by oil.

Cheap and abundant oil and coal have made our prosperity possible. It was the discovery of coal deposits and the technology to use that energy that made the Industrial Revolution possible. Then, the oil boom led to an age of invention. But after 200 years of nonstop oil and coal use, the Earth's limited supply of fossil fuels is running low. Prominent energy expert Richard Heinberg sums it up perfectly: "We are today living at the end of the period of greatest material abundance in human history—an abundance based on temporary sources of cheap energy that made all else possible." Now we must invent a new, better way to live.

We must also stop the damage to our land caused by oil drilling.

"You cannot change the fruits that are already hanging on the tree. You can, however, change tomorrow's fruits. But to do so, you will have to dig below the ground and strengthen the roots."

—T. Harv Eker

In our relentless search for untapped oil reserves, we drill in wilderness areas, threatening the integrity of these unspoiled corners of our planet. Oil tanker accidents spill millions of gallons into the ocean, damaging miles of beaches and killing or injuring so many of the birds, fish and sea mammals that we love.

Oil has been an essential tool in our lives (we drive our cars and we heat our homes with oil). But things must change because the sources are running low, and our fossil fuel dependence is damaging our earth.

Now we must invent a newer, better way to live. Our future must travel a different path than our past.

EXERCISE:
For one day, try to keep track of how much oil-derived energy you use.

AFFIRMATION:
I acknowledge that fossil fuels are finite in supply.

"Americans now spend more money on fast food than on higher education, personal computers, computer software, or new cars. They spend more on fast food than on movies, books, magazines, newspapers, videos, and recorded music—combined."

—ERIC SCHLOSSER

6

THE FOOD THAT NOURISHES

"The word humility (also human) is derived from the Latin humus, meaning 'the soil.' Perhaps this is not simply because it entails stooping and returning to earthly origins, but also because, as we are rooted in this earth of everyday life, we find in it all the vitality and fertility unnoticed by people who merely tramp on across the surface, drawn by distant landscapes."

—PIERO FERRUCCI

FOOD NOURISHES OUR bodies and enriches our lives. Meals, cooking, and cherished recipes bring friends and families together. Food is meaningful to all of us, in many different ways.

No matter what we choose to eat, the food comes to us from our Earth. For this reason, we must respect the bounty of our planet's seasons. It is hard to imagine how our eating habits can have a negative effect on the Earth. But we are coming to learn that our insistence on a varied selection of food, year round, comes with a high environmental price tag.

Much of what we eat today comes to our tables from another climate. Today, walking through the aisles of a grocery store is almost like taking a trip around the world: strawberries from Chile and Asian pears are available in the middle of winter. Americans have come to expect constant variety in their diet, wher-

"He is your needs answered. He is your field which you sow with love and reap with thanksgiving. And He is your board and your fireside. For you come to him with your hunger, and you seek him for peace."

—KAHLIL GIBRAN

ever they live, whatever the time of year. This means we must often import our food from across the country or around the world. It is important to understand how this affects our Earth.

When food has to travel great distances, it is not just shipping that is expensive; the environmental impact is also costly. The true cost of transporting a flat of strawberries from Chile to a grocery store in the United States, for example, must also take into account the manpower, fossil fuel consumption, and carbon emissions required for those strawberries to make their journey from foreign fields to our table.

"Food miles" is the phrase used to designate the number of miles a product must travel in order to reach the consumer. A flat of strawberries from Chile shipped to Ohio has traveled more "food miles" than a flat from California. Experts argue that a measurement of foods impact on the Earth should also take into account *weather* (strawberries grown in hothouses have a bigger carbon footprint

"The love of dirt is among the earliest of passions, as it is the latest . . . Fondness for the ground comes back to a man after he has run the round of pleasure and business. The love of digging in the ground (or of looking on while he pays another to dig) is sure to come back to him, as he is sure, at last, to go under the ground, and stay there."

—CHARLES DUDLEY WARNER

than those grown in sunlight) and *transportation type* (ocean freighters use less fuel than aircraft). "Food miles" are a rough, but crucial, calculation of the environmental impact of our foodstuffs that can help us assess the full costs of our food choices.

When we think in terms of food miles, those Chilean strawberries are expensive—even if they cost less than fruit from California—the cost for the environment is high. When our expectations for modern life lead to behavior that is wasteful, and ultimately unsustainable, we must make a change for the Earth.

EXERCISE:

At your next meal, consider where each food item came from. Try to identify the sources.

AFFIRMATION:

The food I eat sustains and nourishes me.

"Earth's warming climate is estimated to contribute to more than 150,000 deaths and 5 million illnesses each year, according to the World Health Organization, a toll that could double by 2030."

—WORLD HEALTH ORGANIZATION

OUR PLANET CANNOT protect us if we do not protect our planet's atmosphere.

Beyond the clouds, our Earth is surrounded by "greenhouse gases," layers of elements like carbon dioxide, methane, and nitrous oxide. Together, these gases form a protective layer over our planet. It is important that these gases exist together in the right amounts. Otherwise, when that balance is disrupted, we experience global warming. This imbalance can raise average temperatures and cause rapid climate change.

What can cause the imbalance that leads to global warming? For one, the worldwide increase in carbon emissions from the burning of fossil fuels. The industrial boom occurring in China, India, and other developing countries worldwide is contributing to dangerous levels of pollution.

Global warming means our Earth's delicate equilibrium is being thrown out of balance. Increased average temperatures have

"Earth, my dearest. Oh
believe me, you no longer
need your springtimes to win
me over . . . Unspeakably, I
have belonged to you, from
the first."

—RAINER MARIA RILKE

been blamed for shrinking polar ice caps, heat waves, droughts, and wildfires, as well as fierce tropical typhoons and hurricanes.

Experts agree that global warming is one of the most profound threats of our time. We must do everything in our power to guard the fragile balance of Earth's atmosphere.

EXERCISE:
Walk outside and experience the climate. Is a breeze brushing your cheek? Is the sun warm on your skin? How does it feel to you?

AFFIRMATION:
I acknowledge that my choices today have a long term impact on the Earth's climate.

A Prayer for the World

BY
AMY POWERS, ROB WELLS
AND CHARLENE GILLIAM

Can you imagine
Just for one moment in time
Every soul that's on this earth
Finds the silence
To go to that deep place inside
Where we know what life is worth

If we can only reconnect
The joy of what we have
Forget the things that we can't do
And just do what we can

"Action expresses priorities."

—Mahatma Gandhi

7 SIMPLE WAYS

"We need to rediscover the vast, harmonious, pattern of the natural world we are a part of—the infinite complexity and variety of its components, the miraculous simplicity of the whole."

—JAMES RAMSEY ULLMAN

YOU

CAN SAVE THE EARTH

In the course of a single day, every one of us makes hundreds of decisions. Many of these choices have an impact on our environment. Choices like: should I ride the bus or take my car? Should I shop at a local store or drive to the mall?

Make the effort to learn how to make better choices for our environment. Many of these choices are small and simple—yet powerful.

Change can be difficult, especially when life is so hectic. But when it comes to protecting our Earth for the future, change is essential. The choices we make today will shape the future of our Earth. The

"Love the earth and sun and the animals . . . read these leaves in the open air every season of every year of your life."

—WALT WHITMAN

∾

future will be determined by the choices we make now, in our own homes, towns, and cities. Every time we make a decision, we have an opportunity to protect our environment. And although it may be difficult at first, it is only change that can alter the course of history.

Begin today.

". . . . when you work you fulfill
a part of earth's furthest dream,
assigned to you when that
dream was born, And in keeping
yourself with labour you are in
truth loving life, And to love life
through labor is to be intimate
with life's inmost secret."

—KAHLIL GIBRAN

1

LOVE THE EARTH

"It really boils down to this: that all life is interrelated. We are all caught in an inescapable network of mutuality, tied into a single garment of destiny. Whatever affects one directly, affects all indirectly."

—MARTIN LUTHER KING, JR.

BEFORE WE CAN effectively change our actions, we must change our mindset. In everything we do, we must act out of love for the Earth. In the same way that you love a child, a friend, a family member, or anyone special in your life, you must also love the Earth. Your love requires thoughtfulness and action.

What does it mean to "love the Earth?" It means taking the time to think about what would protect our environment—and what might harm it—before we act. This is called "Earth-strategizing."

To Earth-strategize is to seek opportunities for personal practices that are Earth conscious. Here is an example. When you have a chore to do outside, like clearing the lawn of leaves, choose to rake instead of using your leaf blower. In this way, you are protecting the environment, and also using that time to appreciate the season's gifts. Our lives often move too fast for us to take the time to notice

"The sun, the moon and the stars would have disappeared long ago . . . had they happened to be within the reach of predatory human hands."

—HAVELOCK ELLIS

the wonder of the Earth. But we can make the time, and help our environment, too.

Another part of Earth strategizing is practicing waste awareness. Simply put, this means being aware of the amount of waste we generate on a daily basis, and trying to cut it down. This can mean little things, like grabbing less paper napkins, skipping the ATM receipt, or bringing your own mug to work instead of using the disposable cups. Once you start to practice waste awareness, you will look at things differently. The next time you open a package, you will be shocked by the amount of plastic, cardboard, and other materials that surround the contents. You will realize that after you open the package, all that material is useless, and you will suspect that such excessive packaging does not make good use of our resources or our planet. And you will be right.

The Environmental Protection Agency suggests that packaging constitutes as much as one-third of the solid waste generated by individuals and households.

"We abuse land because we regard it as a commodity belonging to us. When we see land as a community to which we belong, we may begin to use it with love and respect."

—ALDO LEOPOLD

What can you do to lower that statistic? Well, next time you need an item, look into purchasing it closer to home. Because ours is a small, blue planet with limited resources. We must protect it by restricting the amount of waste we generate.

Earth-strategizing and making good use of the Earth can be tricky at first, but once we get used to it, it will seem obvious and natural. Whatever the activity, there is an Earth-friendly way to do it. If each one of us Earth-strategizes each and every day, we can move mountains.

We can become generous towards the Earth. We can learn to seek opportunities to make choices that are good for our Earth.

EXERCISE:
See in your mind Earth as a living thing worthy of love.

AFFIRMATION:
I love my life, I love my Earth.

"To see a world in a grain of sand,
And a heaven in a wild flower,
Hold infinity in the palm of your
hand,
And eternity in an hour."

—WILLIAM BLAKE

2

MAKE WISER CHOICES

"There are two ways to get enough: one is to continue to accumulate more and more. The other is to desire less."

—G.K. Chesterton

OUR LIVES ARE made up of many choices. With these choices come responsibility. We can choose to make better choices about what we buy and how we live. And we have a responsibility to do so. As a consumer, you are powerful: you decide what to buy and what companies to support. If you choose healthy and Earth-friendly products, manufacturers will supply them to us—and they will be cheaper—it is simply supply and demand.

Our best choices are made when we are informed. Make an effort to learn how your product got to the store. This means knowing who makes or grows the item, and where. How do we make organic, biodegradable, recycled, and Earth-friendly goods readily available and inexpensive? When it comes to food, this means becoming educated, responsible consumers.

The next time you shop, think carefully. Keep in mind the often-excessive food miles

"The secrets of this earth are not for all men to see, but only for those who will seek them."

—Ayn Rand

some of our imported food must travel to reach our stores. That knowledge will raise a red flag when you come across those imported strawberries in the supermarket, and you will look for strawberries that are locally grown, or choose another fruit that is local and in season.

Keep learning. Research and understand the origins and practices that delivered that box of cereal or package of bacon to the grocery store. Maybe the company that processed that bacon has been accused of unsanitary practices. Are you going to buy the bacon, no matter how inexpensive it is? No. Also try to understand the manufacturing conditions of the products. How environmentally sound is the plant? Does it pollute? The answers to these questions should influence your purchases. Be a responsible, conscientious consumer.

Finally, we also need to be concerned with where our products end up. Phosphates may biodegrade, but they can cause algae blooms when released into streams, rivers, and lakes. And just what does that "biodegradable" label

"And if we do act, in however small a way, we don't have to wait for some grand utopian future. The future is an infinite succession of presents, and to live now as we think human beings should live, in defiance of all that is bad around us, is itself a marvelous victory."

—HOWARD ZINN

mean on your household cleaner? It should mean that the cleaner contains organic ingredients that decompose easily.

Try the new green products. If they work for you, try some more. When it comes to saving the Earth, each individual initiative adds up, and is a step in the right direction. Pretty soon, it'll get harder and harder to find non-Earth-friendly products on the shelves.

Remember, you wield immense power as a consumer.

EXERCISE:
Replace your cleaning products as well as soaps, detergents, and shampoos with Earth-friendly ones. If you don't understand the ingredients on a product label, don't buy it.

AFFIRMATION:
When I choose something Earth-friendly, I choose something good for me and my loved ones.

"If civilization has risen from the Stone Age, it can rise again from the Wastepaper Age."

—JACQUES BARZUN

3

CHOOSE TO
REDUCE

"Do not wait for leaders. Do it alone, person to person."

—MOTHER TERESA

WE MUST CHOOSE to reduce our use of fossil fuels.

Why? For one, fossil fuels like oil and coal are nonrenewable resources. *Nonrenewable* means we cannot replace what we've used; once its consumed, it's gone for good. Second, the burning of fossil fuels for energy damages our environment.

We burn fossil fuels to drive our cars and light our homes-two of our major basic needs. The majority of all that energy is provided by fossil fuels. We must use less of this energy.

When we burn fossil fuels to produce energy, we generate massive quantities of gases, like carbon dioxide, that throw off the balance in our atmosphere.

We will have to change our habits. Right now, our modern way of life is organized around the car. Automobile exhaust is 95% carbon dioxide. This means that the typical passenger vehicle produces over 5 metric tons

"The earth we abuse and the living things we kill will, in the end, take their revenge; for in exploiting their presence we are diminishing our future."

—MARYA MANNES

of carbon dioxide per year. We need to reduce our car habit.

Carpooling is one solution. Sharing a ride with co-workers can be a fun opportunity to chat. Taking the bus is another way to get out and make your solitary commute a social occasion. Some people vow to take the bus on nice days to cut down on driving days—and to get some exercise to and from the bus stop as well. And the more people taking the bus or train, the more the routes and schedules will reflect where and when we want to travel.

For shorter distances, there is nothing better than walking. Consider shopping closer to home. Many of our small towns and cities have at least a shop or two that provide essentials and are just a walk away. Often, we overlook these smaller stores for the bigger ones because larger chains offer more "deals." But how much money do we *really* save in the end by driving to a huge store? The trip itself will cost us gas money; not to mention the fact that a store with huge selection may tempt us into buying more than

"Each and every master, regardless of the era or the place, heard the call and attained harmony with heaven and earth. There are many paths leading to the top of Mount Fuji, but there is only one summit—love."

—MORIHEI UESHIBA

we need. Riding a bike to the store is also a great solution.

So next time, try walking or riding to a local store to pick up that carton of eggs. You will save yourself time and the headache of waiting in traffic and looking for a parking spot. You'll see the sights. And you'll get some exercise, too!

What we hope is that if we look a little closer at things, we just might find answers that will not only improve the Earth, but change our lives, too. By rethinking our priorities, we can rediscover a pace of life that is slower, more localized, more community-oriented. A way of life that is better for us, and better for the Earth.

EXERCISE:
Make a short list of ways you can reduce your dependency on fossil fuel.

AFFIRMATION:
I am committed to doing my part to conserve limited energy resources.

"The system of nature, of which man is a part, tends to be self-balancing, self-adjusting, self-cleansing. Not so with technology."

—E.F. Schumacher

4

EMBRACE GREEN TECHNOLOGY

"Humanity is on the march,
earth itself is left behind."

—David Ehrenfeld

OUR FUTURE WILL be built on "green" technology.

That future is here now.

More and more, manufacturers around the world are using technological innovation to make products work more on less energy.

Take this simple example: the light bulb. The traditional incandescent light bulb requires a lot of energy to light a room—and wastes a lot of energy, too—90 percent of the energy burned is wasted as heat. Because of this, Congress recently passed legislation that will phase out the incandescent light bulb by 2010, and replace it with compact fluorescent bulbs, called CFLs. Compact fluorescents use 75 percent less energy than incandescent bulbs *and* last longer.

You might hear "fluorescent lighting" and automatically think of your office, the gym, or a doctor's office. But CFL lighting is very sophisticated, ranging from bright white to

"A margin of life is developed by Nature for all living things—including man. All life forms obey Nature's demands—except man, who has found ways of ignoring them."

—EUGENE M. POIROT

warm, like incandescent light. The bottom line is, by replacing our centuries-old incandescent bulbs, we can reduce our consumption of electricity and immediately reduce our carbon emissions. All that with only a twist of the wrist!

Every product you buy presents an opportunity for you to conserve energy and embrace green technology. Appliances like microwaves, washers, dryers, and air conditioners can all be found with an energy-saving logo—you just have to get out there and look for them.

There are other, more long-term ways to save energy as well. One is reinsulating and resealing your home. By adding insulation in the attic, or in crawlspaces and replacing old-single paned windows with double-paned models, you can save substantially on your utility bills. You can also make changes to your hot-water heater. About 15 percent of an average home energy bill goes to heating water. By turning down the temperature of your hot water, insulating the tank, and replacing old heaters with more energy-

"I realized that Eastern thought had somewhat more compassion for all living things. In the East, the wilderness has no evil connotation; it is thought of as an expression of the unity and harmony of the universe."

—WILLIAM O. DOUGLAS

efficient models, the average family can save energy and reduce their monthly fuel bills—and, in some states, get a tax rebate or other incentive.

Heating and cooling our homes accounts for 45 percent of our monthly utility bills. So turn down the thermostat during the winter, and in hot weather, draw the blinds or curtains, open the windows on the shady side of the house—and if you don't have shade, plant some trees. They will also protect your house from harsh winter winds. Every degree warmer or cooler represents big savings both for you and the planet. Green energy is the key to our future. Embrace it now.

EXERCISE:

Conduct a survey of your home and discover where you can apply green technology to conserve.

AFFIRMATION:

I will choose energy and resource-saving technology.

"We live in the world, and the
world lives in us."

—ALBERT SCHWEITZER

❧

5

RECYCLE, REUSE, REPAIR

"What we choose to emphasize in this complex history will determine our lives. If we see only the worst, it destroys our capacity to do something. If we remember those times and places...where people have behaved magnificently, it energizes us to act, and raises at least the possibility of sending this... world in a different direction."

—HOWARD ZINN

WE HAVE A responsibility to the Earth to use our resources carefully.

One way to do this is by recycling. We can also get the most out of what we own by repairing appliances and products so they last, instead of buying new ones. We can also reuse items, like boxes, for other purposes.

By now, most of us are familiar with the importance of recycling. Hopefully, we do it without even thinking. But just because it has become second nature to most of us shouldn't blind us to the fact that recycling is making a major difference. If anything, the way recycling has become a part of our everyday lives should be an example of how to incorporate other environmentally-minded changes into our lifestyles.

Time has shown that recycling works. Since the 1970s, recycling programs have made use of literally tons of discarded material. Imagine: so-called garbage was successfully

"It appears to be a law that you cannot have a deep sympathy with both man and nature."

—HENRY DAVID THOREAU

❧

made useful again—instead of just taking up room in a dump.

Did you know that the business of recycling is profitable, too? For one, it contributes to a healthy job market. It is estimated that sorting and recycling discarded materials generates 5 to 10 times as many jobs as conventional waste disposal. The Office of the Federal Environmental Executive estimates that recycling and remanufacturing industries account for approximately 1 million manufacturing jobs and more than $100 billion in revenue. Companies are increasingly discovering that the cost of recycling is matched by profit earned from manufacturing with reused materials, rather than using new, raw materials exclusively. Increasingly, recycled materials are even becoming significantly cheaper to use than new materials.

Our individual recycling efforts can have major positive results. Example: the plastic bag. One estimate holds that the average American uses between 300 and 700 plastic

"Time and space—time to be alone, space to move about—these may well become the great scarcities of tomorrow."

—EDWIN WAY TEALE

bags each year. In the U.S., plastic and paper bag production requires some 12 million barrels of oil and 14 million trees each year. By recycling or reusing plastic and paper bags, we can cut into those numbers significantly. Many shoppers are either bringing plastic bags back to the grocery store to reuse or are bringing their own cloth bags. It won't be long before we may no longer see stray plastic bags fluttering in the branches of trees.

In addition to recycling, we can reuse and repair. This is easier than you might think. Imagine how much plastic you'll conserve, and how much money you'll save, by using refillable glass containers for water instead of buying water in plastic bottles. Or you can start using washable dishtowels instead of paper towels. Be less wasteful.

We just have to change the way we think. Historically, people raised during tough times knew how to make due. Many individuals who were raised during the Great Depression pride themselves on their ability to fix *anything*, and reuse common items

"The miracle is not to walk on water. The miracle is to walk on the green earth in the present moment, to appreciate the peace and beauty that are available now."

—THICH NHAT HANH

that the rest of us would throw away, such as using the bags that baked bread comes in for plastic baggies. The wasteful habits we are trying to change are recent ones, and we can overcome them by remembering and honoring our parents' and grandparents' resourceful ways of living.

Recycling, reusing and repairing are part of a simple shift in our behavior that will change our impact on the Earth.

EXERCISE:

Consider all the material possessions you own. Choose to take as much care as needed to extend the life of these items. Within the next month, sew a tear, pass on unneeded items to others, and find ways to encourage recycling at home or at work.

AFFIRMATION:

I will be mindful of the goods I buy and keep.

"We are the ones we have
been waiting for."

—JUNE JORDAN

6

THINK LOCAL

"The land and sea, the animals, fishes, and birds, the sky of heaven and the orbs, the forests, mountains, and rivers, are not small themes."

—WALT WHITMAN

WHAT DOES IT mean to think local? "Local" means you can walk or ride a bike or bus to wherever you need to go. "Local" means less energy consumed, and therefore fewer carbon emissions. "Local" means being kinder to our planet.

As large as our world has grown, it's often still possible to find everything we need within miles of our homes. All we have to do is look.

Why is "local" better for the planet? When you buy locally, you save energy. But just as importantly, you promote regional farmers and businesses . . . which means you're helping to build a stronger community. How can you buy local? Farmers markets and food stands are springing up all across the country, and are a perfect opportunity to find some really great produce and meet the man or woman who grew the tomato or gathered the egg you're buying. Knowing the people

"We shall never achieve harmony with land, any more than we shall achieve absolute justice or liberty for people. In these higher aspirations, the important thing is not to achieve but to strive."

—ALDO LEOPOLD

who help put food on your table also builds a stronger community.

Buying locally also means that the food you serve your family will be fresh, in season, and unique to the region you live in. Many cooks will tell you that it is wonderful to have access to imported tomatoes in the middle of winter. But they will also admit those imported tomatoes do not taste anything like the tomatoes from your local farmers market in the summer. Buying food locally usually means quality you can see and taste.

There's a saying that all politics is local. We think this means that no matter what they say or do in our state capitols or Washington, it's how we deal with issues in our own backyards that will make a change. "Local" means community. So support your local community organizations. When we think, buy, live, and act locally, we strengthen our community—and it is as a community, working together, that we will save the Earth.

"When we try to pick out anything by itself, we find it hitched to everything else in the Universe."

—John Muir

EXERCISE:

Take one week to discover local sources for your daily needs: food, entertainment, services, and other necessities and tasks.

AFFIRMATION:

I choose to be aware of the myriad opportunities to meet my needs within my community.

"What would the world
be, once bereft
Of wet and of wildness?
Let them be left,
O let them be left, wildness
and wet;
Long live the weeds and the
wilderness yet."

—GERARD MANLEY HOPKINS

7

CHERISH THE EARTH'S PRECIOUS GIFTS

"We never know the worth of water till the well is dry."

—THOMAS FULLER

EACH OF US must play our own part in helping to save the Earth.

As you work toward making a difference, remember why you want to save our planet: perhaps it's the simple joy you feel in the taste of fresh water, or in the touch of a sweet smelling breeze. Or maybe it's the sense of solidarity you feel with the Earth when you look at an awe-inspiring landscape unspoiled by human development.

So how can you cherish the Earth?

Look outside your home. Whether you live in the country, the suburbs, or the city, seek air, trees, grass, and sun. Embrace the explorer within by taking a road you've never been down just to see where it leads. Go for a hike with your kids or a friend, or ride your bike to a neighboring town. Plan a vacation to the seashore to learn about creatures great and small, from whales to the tiny life forms that dwell in tidal pools.

"Man has been endowed with reason, with the power to create, so that he can add to what he's been given. But up to now he hasn't been a creator, only a destroyer. Forests keep disappearing, rivers dry up, wild life's become extinct, the climate's ruined and the land grows poorer and uglier every day."

—ANTON CHEKHOV

On the weekend, wake up early on Saturday and go fishing. You may not catch anything, but you'll be able to watch mist rise off the fields as the sun comes up.

Look in your own backyard, too. You can plant a vegetable garden or even fill planters with flowers. If you live in a big city, join a community garden. Even home improvements can be meaningful. Build a tire swing for your grandkids or contribute one to your local park, so kids can swing and pretend to touch the sky.

We know more about our Earth and its wonders than we ever have, and we are discovering more all the time. All our knowledge should only make us more protective, and more awestruck, at the beauty of our home. This great planet has most value in the human eye and heart. So explore the woods. Lay in the grass and watch the clouds gather overhead. Hike to the top of a hill and breathe deeply.

No matter what form your connection to our planet may take, the importance of the

"To find the universal elements enough;
to find the air and the water exhilarating; to be refreshed by a morning walk or an evening saunter; to be thrilled by the stars at night;
to be elated over a bird's nest or a wildflower in spring—these are some of the rewards of the simple life."

—JOHN BURROUGHS

relationship between humans and the Earth is undeniable, and must never be forgotten.

We will save the Earth by loving it.

EXERCISE:

The next time you take a walk, take a hike, go for a bike ride, or go for a swim, bring a friend or family member along. Enjoy the day. Talk about what you see in nature around you. Smile. You are alive!

AFFIRMATION:

Feel gratitude for the Earth's resources in everything you do. Say, "thank you."

A Special Thank You

You've reached the last page of this little book—now it is up to you to write the next chapter. Take the lessons you have learned here and share your discoveries with others. Be a force for sustainability in your home, community, and workplace. Choose to lend a hand, plant a tree, and make a difference.

Andrew Flach, Publisher
June Eding, Editor
Ryan Tumambing, Associate Publisher
Anna Krusinski, Associate Editor
Sean Smith, Writer

NOTES

Ueshiba, Morihei, *Art of Peace: Teachings of the Founder of Aikido.* (Shambhala Pubns., 1993).

Leopold, Aldo, *A sand country almanac: with other essays on conservation from round river.* (Oxford University Press, 1966).

7 REASONS WHY

Harney, Corbin, *The way it is: one water—one air—one mother earth.* (Nevada City, CA: Blue Dolphin Pub., 1995).

INTRODUCTION TO PART 1

Abbey, Edward, *Desert Solitaire: A Season in the Wilderness.* (New York: McGraw-Hill, 1968).

Yeats, William Butler, "The Municipal Gallery Revisited," in *Collected Poems.* (London: Macmillan, 1955).

CHAPTER 1

Bresette, Walter, "7th Generation Initiative" http://www. protecttheearth.net/Walter/aboutwalt7.htm (accessed 7/31/08).

McMichael, A. J, *Climate change and human health: risks and responses.* (Geneva: World Health Organization, 2003).

Bradsher, Keith andBarboza, David, "Pollution From Chinese Coal Casts a Global Shadow," *The New York Times,* June 11, 2006.

Whitehead, Alfred North, *Science and the modern world. Lowell lectures, 1925.* (New York: Macmillan Co., 1925).

Royt, Elizabeth, "From Bad to Thirst: How the Nation's Breadbasket is Poisoning Its Own Water Supply," *Grist,* October 16, 2007.

Harris, Marjorie, *In the garden: thoughts on the changing seasons.* (Toronto: HarperCollins Publishers, 1995).

CHAPTER 2

Emerson, Ralph Waldo. "The American Scholar." *The Essential Writings of Ralph Waldo Emerson*. Ed. Brooks Atkinson. (Modern Library, 2000).

McMichael, A. J. *Climate change and human health: risks and responses*. (Geneva: World Health Organization, 2003).

"Effects of Global Environmental Change on Human Health," *ScienceDaily*, November 15, 2006, http://www.sciencedaily.com/releases/2005/11/061113170814.htm.

White, E. B. *Essays of E.B. White*. (New York: Harper & Row, 1977).

Gore, Al. "Speech On the Acceptance of the Nobel Peace Prize" (December 10, 2007).

CHAPTER 3

Jacques Cousteau, "We forget that the water cycle and the life cycle are one."

Pascal, B., *Thoughts on religion, and other subjects*. (London: Thomas Tegg and Son, 1836).

Pacific Institute, "Fact Sheet: Bottled Water and Energy: Getting 17 Million Barrels," 2007, http://www.pacinst.org/topics/integrity_of_science/case_studies/bottled_water_factsheet.pdf.

Ibid.

Peter Gleick, quoted in Tom Paulson, "Thirst For Bottled Water May Hurt Environment," *Seattle Post-Intelligencer*, April 19, 2007.

Gilpin, Laura, *The Rio Grande, river of destiny: an interpretation of the river, the land, and the people*. (New York: Duell, Sloan and Pearce, 1949).

Natural Resources Defense Council, "Eco-Facts," *2002*, http://www.ecocycle.org/pdfs/Eco-facts_2004.pdf.

Borland, Hal. *Sundial of the seasons*. (Philadelphia: Lippincott, 1964).

CHAPTER 4

Muir, John, and Linnie Marsh Wolfe. *John of the mountains; the unpublished journals of John Muir.* (Boston: Houghton, Mifflin, 1938)

Berry, Thomas Mary, *The dream of the earth.* (San Francisco: Sierra Club Books, 1988).

Greene, David Lloyd, *Reducing greenhouse gas emissions from U.S. transportation.* (Arlington, VA: Pew Center on Global Climate Change, 2003).

American Lung Association, "State of the Air: 2004," http://lungaction.org/reports/sota04exec_summ.html.

U.S. Environmental Protection Agency, "Emission Facts: Greenhouse Gas Emissions from a Typical Passenger Vehicle" (object name EPA420-F-05–004), February 2005, http://www.epa.gov/oms/climate/420f05004.htm#step6.

Shakespeare, William, *Hamlet.* (New York: W.W. Norton & Co., 1996).

Energy Information Administration, "Emission of Greenhouse Gases Report" (object name DOE/EIA-0573), 2006, http://www.eia.doe.gov/oiaf/1605/ggrpt/carbon.html#total.

Berry, Wendell, *The gift of good land: further essays, cultural and agricultural.* (San Francisco: North Point Press, 1981).

CHAPTER 5

Lovins, Amory B. ,"Ending Our Oil Dependence," *The Ripon Forum* Volume 39, Number II (March/April 2005), p. 12.

Brouwer, L.E.J. ,"Growth Despite Shortage" in *TIME* (Monday, May 4, 1970).

Richard Heinberg, "Peak Everything," *Museletter*, No.185, September 2007, http://www.richardheinberg.com/museletter/185.

Eker, T. Harv., *Secrets of the millionaire mind: mastering the inner game of wealth.*(New York: HarperBusiness, 2005).

CHAPTER 6

Schlosser, Eric, *Fast Food Nation: The Dark Side of the All-American Meal* (New York: Houghton Mifflin Co., 2001), p. 3.

Ferrucci, Piero. *Inevitable grace: breakthroughs in the lives of great men and women : guides to your self-realization.* (Los Angeles: J.P. Tarcher, 1990).

Gibran, Kahlil. *The Prophet.* (New York: Knopf, 1952).

Warner, Charles Dudlley. *My summer in a garden.* (London: Sampson, Low, Marston & Co., 1883).

CHAPTER 7

IPCC, *Climate Change 2007: The Physical Science Basis. Contribution of Working Group I to the Fourth Assessment Report of theIntergovernmental Panel on Climate Change.* Solomon,S., D. Qin, M. Manning, Z. Chen, M. Marquis, K.B. Averyt, M.Tignor and H.L. Miller (eds.)]. (United Kingdom and New York, CambridgeUniversity Press, 2007).

McMichael, A. J. *Climate change and human health: risks and responses.* (Geneva: World Health Organization, 2003).

Eilperin, Juliet, "Climate Shift Tied To 150,000 Fatalities: Most Victims Are Poor, Study Says,"*Washington Post* (November 17, 2005).

Rainer Maria Rilke, *Duineser Elegien: Elegies from the Castle of Duino*, trans. V. Sackville-West. (Hogarth Press, London, 1931).

7 SIMPLE WAYS

Mahatma Gandhi, "Action expresses priorities."

INTRODUCTION TO PART 2

Ullman, James Ramsey. *The Age of Mountaineering*. (Philadelphia: Lippincott, 1954).

Whitman, Walt. *Leaves of grass: including Sands at seventy, 1st annex, Goodbye my fancy, 2nd annex, A backward glance o'er travel's roads.* (Philadelphia: D. McKay, 1855).

CHAPTER 1

Gibran, Kahlil. *The Prophet*. (New York: Knopf, 1952).

King, Jr., Martin Luther. "Remaining Awake Through a Great Revolution"(Speech, March 31, 1968) in Clayborne Carson and Peter Holloran, eds. *A Knock at Midnight: Inspiration from the Great Sermons of Reverend Martin Luther King, Jr.* (New York: Warner Books, 1998).

Ellis, Havelock. *The dance of life.* (Boston: Houghton Mifflin Company, 1923).

U.S. Environmental Protection Agency, "Product Stewardship: Packaging," July 10, 2007, http://www.epa.gov/epr/products/packaging.htm.

South Bayside Waste Management Authority, "Quick & Easy May Not Be Worth It: The Cost of Convenience,"2007, http://rethinkwaste.org/news.php?id=costofconvenience.

Leopold, Aldo. *A Sand County Almanac, and sketches here and there.* (New York: Oxford University Press, 1989).

CHAPTER 2

Blake, William. "Auguries of Innocence" in The Pickering Manuscript. (c. 1803)

Chesterton, G. K. *All things considered.* (London: Methuen, 1908).

Rand, Ayn. *Anthem*. (New American Library, 1961).

Zinn, Howard, *A power governments cannot suppress*. (San Francisco: City Lights, 2007) p.170.

CHAPTER 3

Barzun, Jacques. *The house of intellect*. (New York: Harper, 1959).

Mother Theresa, "Do not wait for leaders. Do it alone, person to person."

U.S. Environmental Protection Agency, "Emission Facts: Greenhouse Gas Emissions from a Typical Passenger Vehicle" (object name EPA420-F-05–004), February 2005, http://www.epa.gov/oms/climate/420f05004.htm#step6.

Ibid.

Mannes, Marya. *More in anger*. (Philadelphia: Lippincott, 1958).

Ueshiba, Morihei. *Art of Peace: Teachings of the Founder of Aikido*. (Shambhala Pubns., 1993).

CHAPTER 4

Schumacher, E. F. *Small is beautiful; economics as if people mattered*. (New York: Harper & Row, 1973.

Ehrenfeld, David W. *The arrogance of humanism*. (New York: Oxford University Press, 1978).

U.S. Department of Energy, "Energy Tips: Appliances and Electronics," http://www.doe.gov/applianceselectronics.

Poirot, Eugene M. *Our margin of life*. (New York: Vantage Press, 1964).

ENERGY STAR, "Qualified Residential Light Fixtures,"August 7, 2007, www.energystar.gov/ia/partners/univ/download/Computer_Sell_Sheet.doc.

Alliance to Save Energy, "No-Cost Low-Cost Tips for Saving Money & Energy," 2008, http://www.ase.org/content/article/detail/965.

Douglas, William O. *Go East, young man: the early years; the autobiography of William O. Douglas.* (New York: Random House, 1974).

California Energy Commission, "Consumer Energy Center: Lighting Choices," http://www.consumerenergy-center.org/lighting/index.html.

CHAPTER 5

Schweitzer, Albert. *Thoughts for Our Times.* Edited by Erica Anderson. (The Albert Schweitzer Fellowship, 1975).

Zinn, Howard, *A power governments cannot suppress.* (San Francisco: City Lights, 2007) p.170.

Thoreau, Henry David, and Thomas Carew. *Walden, or, Life in the woods.* (Boston: Ticknor and Fields).

Grassroots Recycling Network, "Create Jobs From Discards," Green Paper no. 3, http://www.grrn.org/resources/grrn3.html.

U.S. Environmental Protection Agency, "Jobs Through Recycling: Economic Benefits," http://www.epa.gov/jtr/econ/index.htm.

Sewell Chan, "Bush's Niece Endorses Plastic Bag Recycling," The New York Times, November 5, 2007.

Teale, Edwin Way. *Autumn across America; a naturalist's record of a 20,000-mile journey through the North American autumn.* (New York: Dodd, Mead, 1956).

Bayside Waste Management, "Waste Redux: Farmers Markets,"http://rethinkwaste.org/news.php?id=wasteredux_farmersmarkets.

Hanh, Thich Nhat. *Touching Peace.* (Parallax Press, 1992) p. 1.

CHAPTER 6

Jordan, June, *Passion: New Poems, 1977–1980.* (Boston: Beacon Press, 1980).

Whitman, Walt. *Leaves of grass: including Sands at seventy, 1st annex, Goodbye my fancy, 2nd annex, A backward glance o'er travel's roads.* (Philadelphia: D. McKay, 1855).

Leopold, Aldo. *A Sand Country Almanac: with other essays on conservation from round river.* (Oxford University Press, 1966).

Muir, John. *My First Summer in the Sierra* (Boston: Houghton Mifflin, 1911).

CHAPTER 7

Hopkins, Gerard Manley. " Inversnaid," *Poems of Gerard Manley Hopkins* (London: Humphrey Milford, 1918).

Fuller, Thomas. *Gnomologia: adagies and proverbs; wise sentences and witty sayings, ancient and modern, foreign and British.* (London: B. Barker; and A. Bettesworth and C. Hitch, 1732).

Chekhov, Anton Pavlovich, Tyrone Guthrie, and Leonid Kipnis. *Uncle Vanya: scenes from country life in four acts.* Minnesota drama editions, no. 5. (Minneapolis: University of Minnesota Press in association with the Minnesota Theatre Co., 1986).

Burroughs, John. *Leaf and tendril.* (Boston: Houghton, Mifflin and Co., 1908).